Coloring Book of Leip

K.S. Bank

Coloring Book of Leipzig, Germany.

Copyright: Published in the United States by K.S. Bank
Published February 2017

ISBN-13: 978-1544891842

ISBN-10: 1544891849

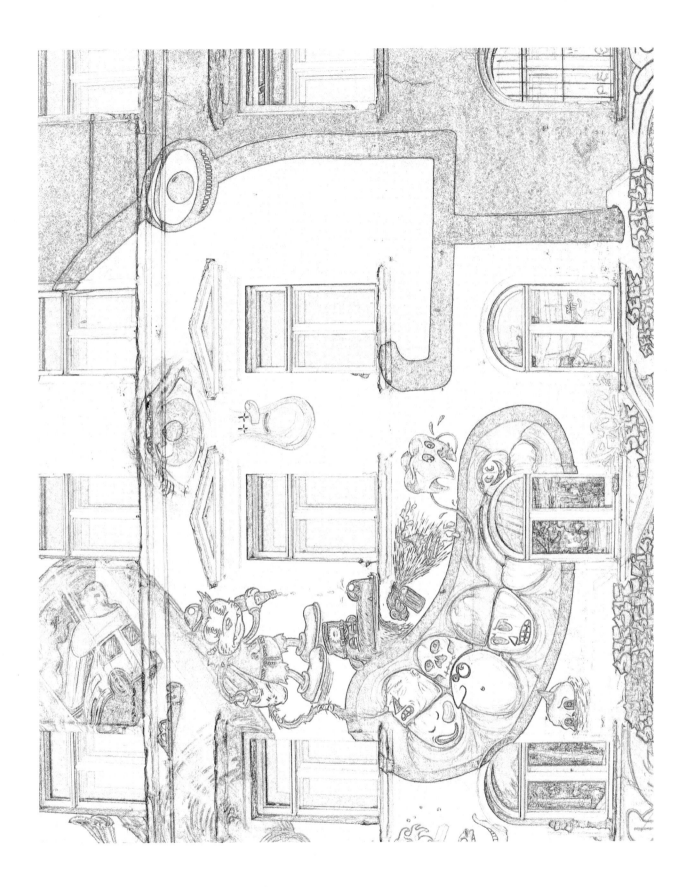

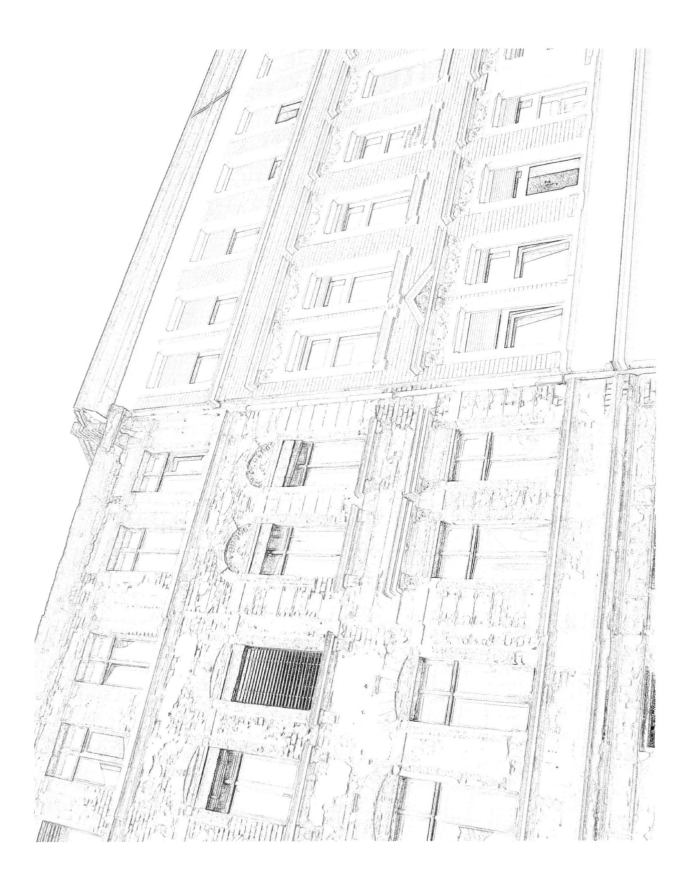

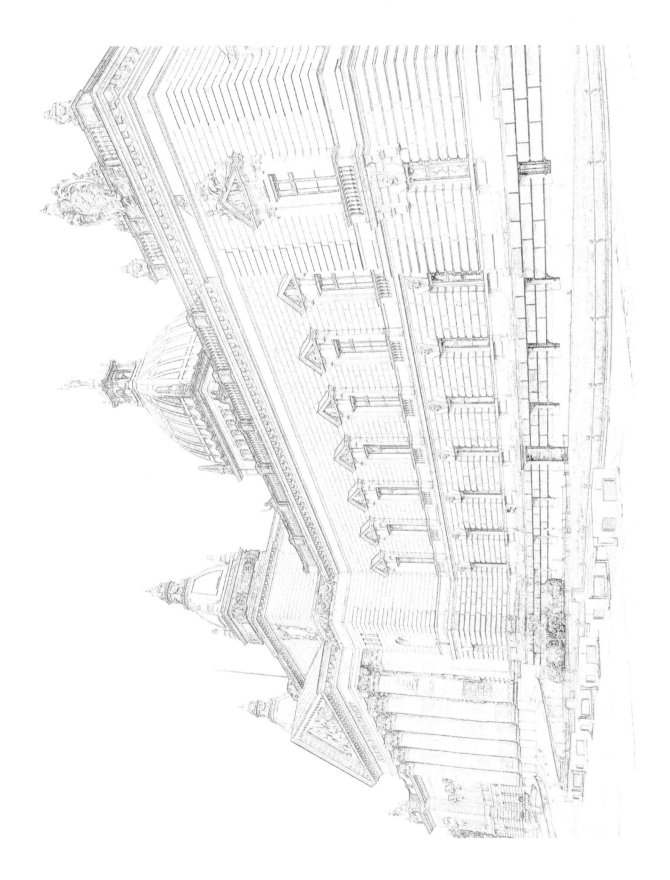

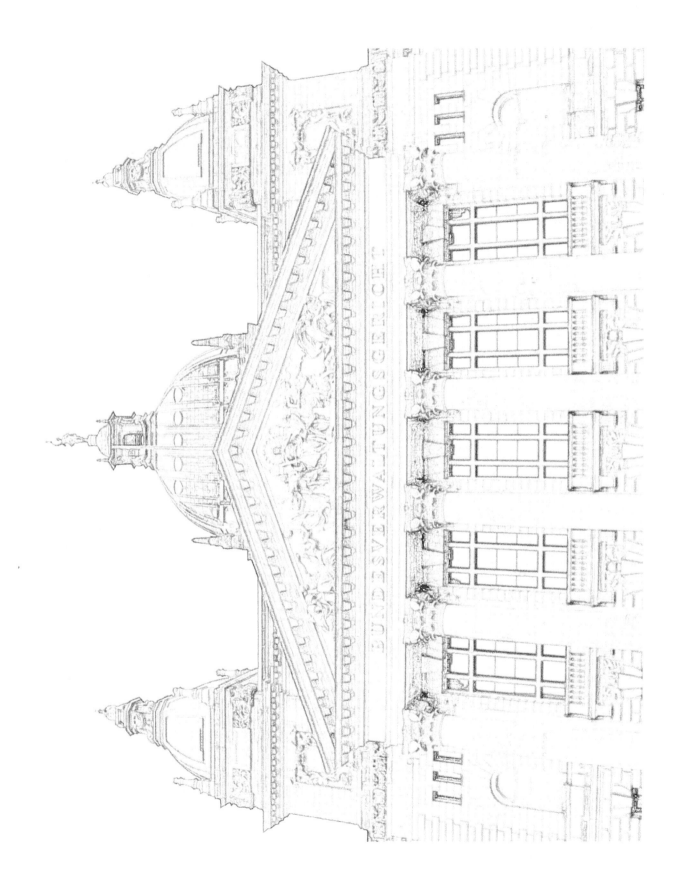

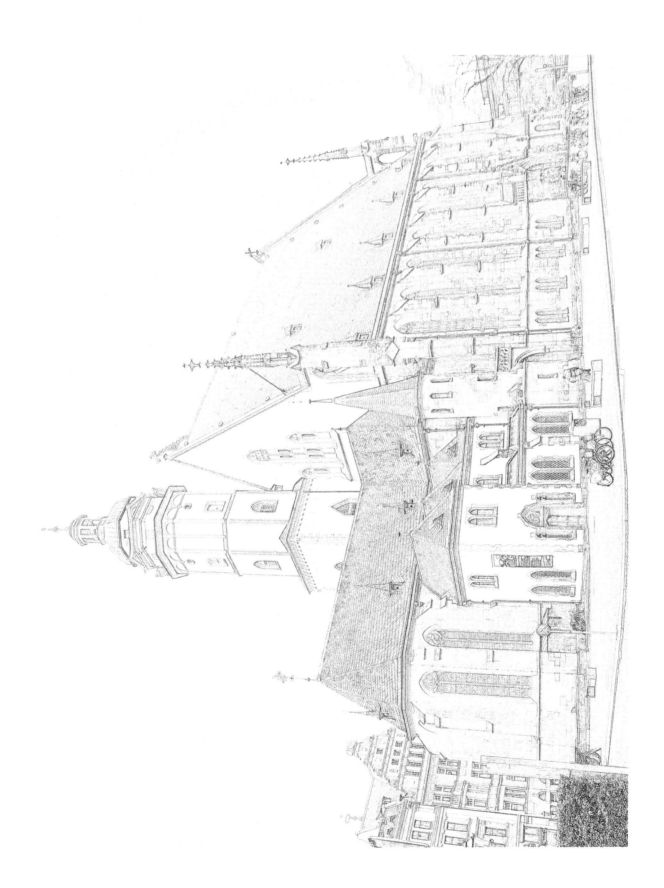

Thank you
K.S. Bank

Made in the USA
Monee, IL
25 April 2022

95332688R10031